A pre-flute course for young beginners

Toot! Toot! Flute

A J Shaw

Begin your flute journey with the fife or recorder

First Published in Australia in 2022

© COPYRIGHT Amelia Jane Shaw 2019

ISBN: 978-0-646-85486-1

All rights reserved. Except as permitted under the Australian Copyright Act 1968 (for example, a fair dealing for the purposes of study, research, criticism or review), no part of this book may be reproduced, stored in a retrieval system, communicated or transmitted in any form or by any means without prior written permission.
All inquiries should be made to the author.

www.toottootflute.com
ameliajshawmusic@gmail.com

Introduction

Toot! Toot! Flute was created to provide a fun engaging method book for younger flautists. This book uses a clear progression that establishes and reinforces key musical concepts in an elementary way.

This method uses a variety of learning techniques from musical games to aural and written activities. Students will journey through an assortment of exercises including traditional songs and original pieces written by the author.

Toot! Toot! Flute is designed to be used with young children who are likely unable to support a full size or curved head flute. For this reason, all material is designed to be played on a fife or recorder in C major.

Children progress through each note, singing and playing songs, until they have learnt a C major scale. This method uses unique coloured note heads to help young children with reading music on the stave. Coloured stickers can also be used as a visual aid to correlate to the keys on their instrument.

Toot! Toot! Flute is suitable for group or individual tuition and is intended to be used in partnership with a teacher.

Contents

Symbols Key	3
Pulse and Rhythm	4
Time Signatures	5
Head Joint Games	8
Breathing	10
Tonguing	11
Mary Had a Little Lamb	12
Beginning to Read Music	13
Let's Get Ready to Play	14
New Note B	17
New Note A	18
New Note G	20
New Note C	30
Articulation	36
New Note F	40
New Note E	44
New Note D	45
New Note Low C	48
The Farmer in the Dell	50
ABC Song	51
Are you Sleeping?	52
Hot Cross Buns	53
Twinkle, Twinkle Little Star	54
On Top of Old Smokey	55
Can Can	55
Brahms Lullaby	56
Baa Baa Black Sheep	57
Old MacDonald	58
Dancing Dinosaurs	59
Singing Sailor	60
Musical Morning	61
Let's Celebrate!	62
Certificate Page	63
Practice Diary	65

Symbols Key

 rhythm time

 take a note

 listen up

 say and play

Pulse and Rhythm

When we play or hear music, we can generally feel a pulse.

This is like the heartbeat of a piece of music. We call this the beat.

 Put your hand on your heart. Do you feel a steady pulse?

How many beats you can feel?

 This is a crotchet. It is worth 1 beat.

It sounds like the word PEAR.

 This is a minim. It is worth 2 beats.

It sounds like the word AP-PLE

𝐨 This is a semibreve. It is worth 4 beats.

It sounds like the word WA-TER-MEL-ON.

Time Signatures

Beats are organised into bars using barlines.

Time signatures tell us how many beats are in a bar.

The top number of the time signature tells us how many beats are in a bar.

The bottom number tells us what type of beat it is.

4/4 means there are 4 crotchet beats in bar.

2/4 means there are 2 crotchet beats in a bar.

Say, then clap these 2/4 rhythms. AS

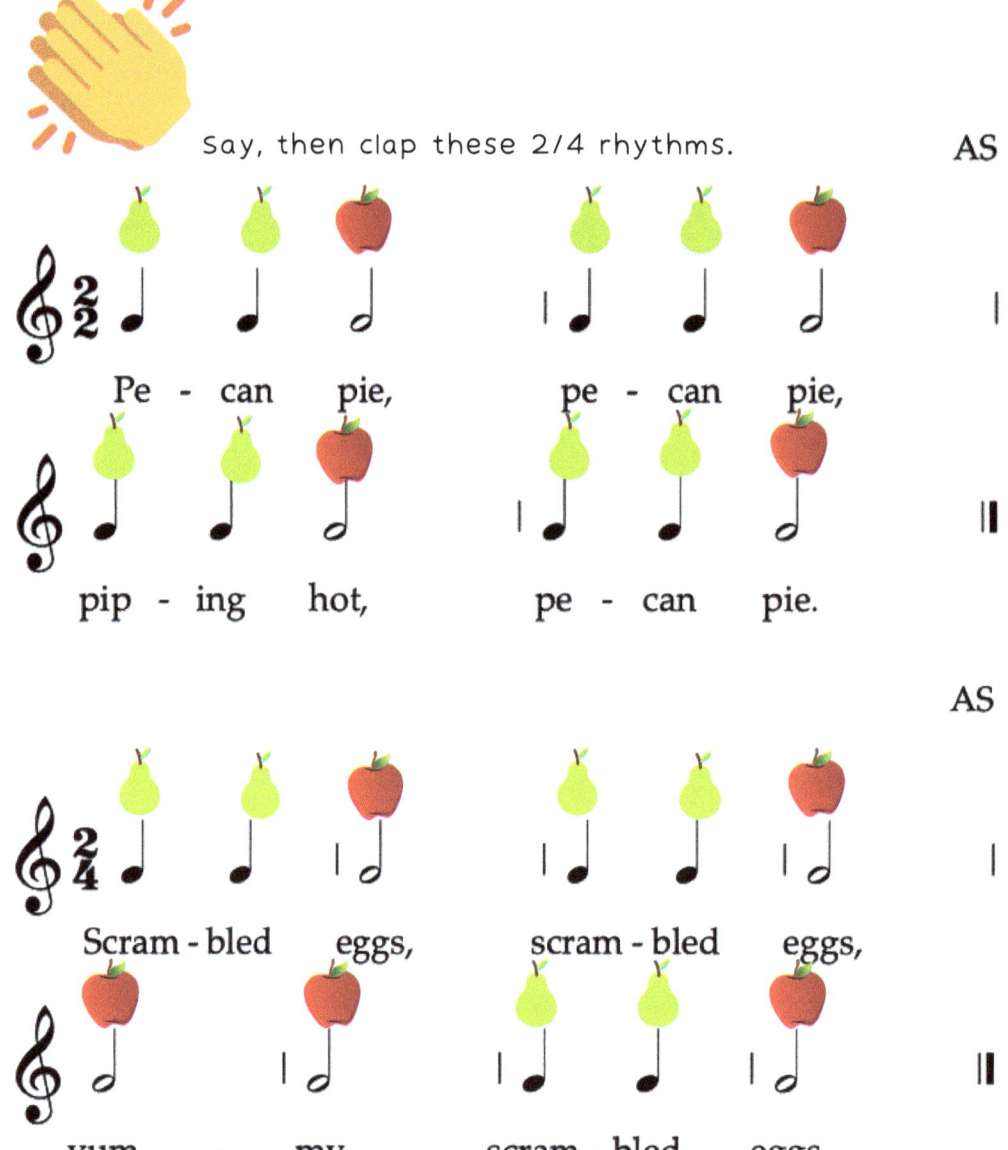

Pe - can pie, pe - can pie,
pip - ing hot, pe - can pie.

AS

Scram - bled eggs, scram - bled eggs,
yum - my, scram - bled eggs.

Try tapping the rhythm as you sing.

- On the first beat tap your head.

- On the second beat tap your shoulders.

- On the third beat tap your knees.

- On the fourth beat tap your toes.

With the help of your teacher complete these rhythms using only crotchets, minims or semibreves.

Now copy your teacher and play these rhythms on the headjoint of your flute.

Remember to always open your flute case on a flat surface!

Head Joint Games

We can make different sounds on the flute depending on how we blow.

The word embouchure refers to the shape of your mouth when you play the flute.

Keeping the corners of your lips together make a tiny whole in the center of your lips and blow over the embouchure hole of the flute.

This is a bit like saying the word 'poo'. When you are blowing in the correct position you will see a small triangle of condensation on the lip plate.

Hold one hand in front of your face.
With your palm at eye level practice blowing as if you were blowing on your flute. You should feel the air on the centre of your palm.

Now see if you can control the airstream blowing from the bottom of your wrist all the way to the tips of your fingers without moving your head.

If that is too easy try blowing all the way down to your elbow.

Blowing on your headjoint, how many ways can you find to change the sound?

Hints...

- Blow with a sad face.
- Blow with a smile.
- Roll the headjoint towards you.
- Roll the headjoint away from you.
- Cover the open end with your palm.
- Slide your finger into the open end.

First practice these exercises with the end of the headjoint covered. Blow harder (pushing from your tummy muscles) to reach the higher notes.

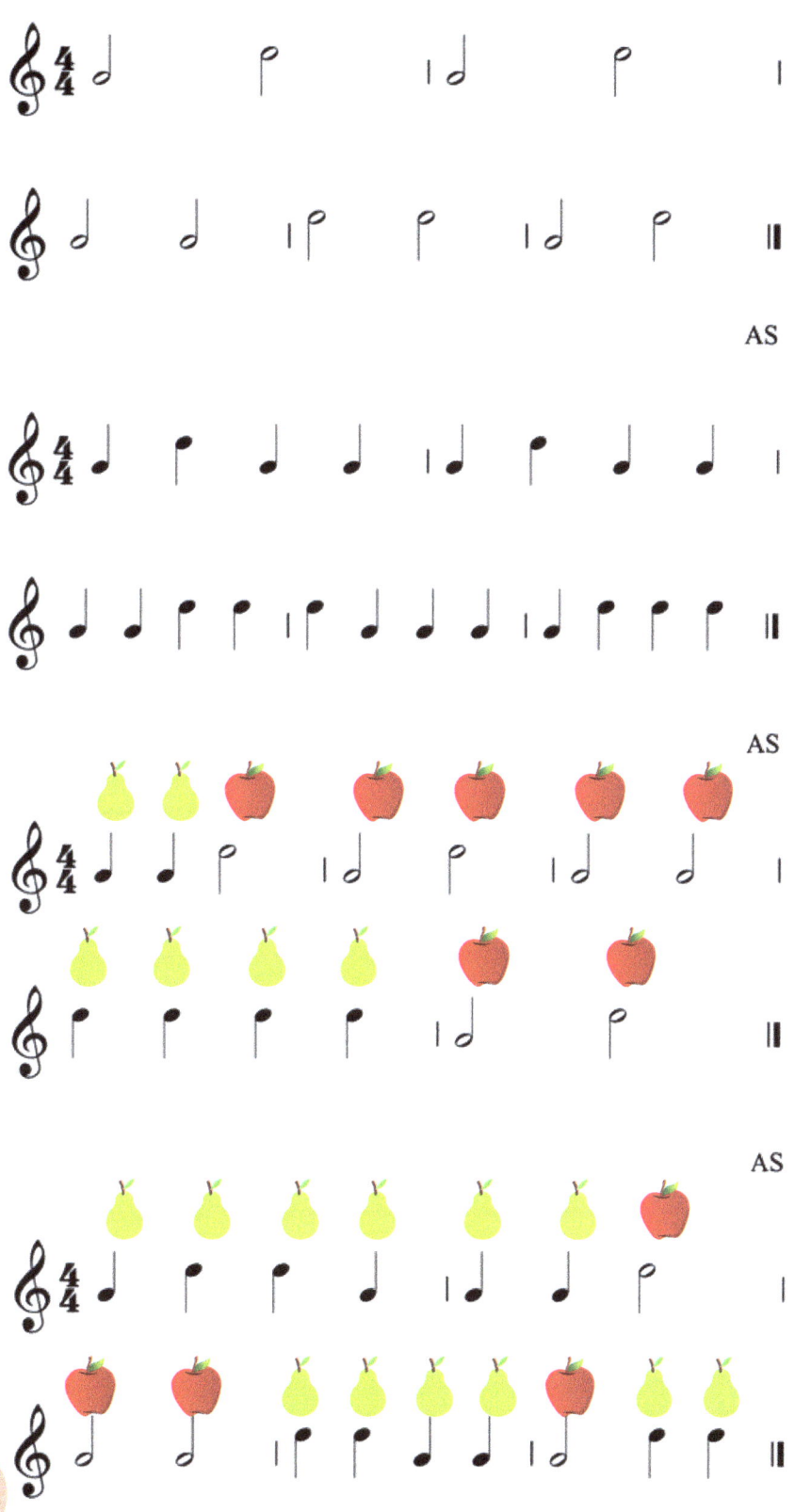

Now try with the end of your headjoint uncovered.

Breathing

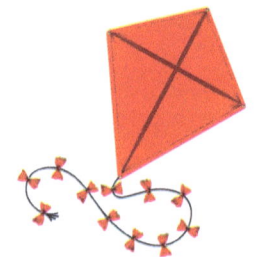

When we play the flute, we need to use special breathing.

1. Keep your shoulders relaxed.

2. Take a big breath in, opening your mouth wide like a yawn.

3. Let your stomach fill up like a balloon.

4. Hold the air and don't let the balloon pop!

5. Squeeze the air out in a hissing snake sound, squeezing from your tummy muscles.

How long can you breathe out for?

Breathe in for 4 beats, then hiss like a snake for 4 beats.
Breathe in for 4 beats, then hiss like a snake for 5 beats.
Breathe in for 4 beats, then hiss like a snake for 6 beats.
Breathe in for 4 beats, then hiss like a snake for 7 beats.
Breathe in for 4 beats, then hiss like a snake for 8 beats.

Can you make it to 10 beats?

Imagine you are blowing a kite up into the air with your breath.

Push from your tummy muscles to send it soaring.

You can use a light piece of paper or tissue paper as the kite.

Tonguing

Every time that you play a note on the flute you should say 'too' at the beginning.

Practise saying 'too, too, too, too' then say 'tootootootoo'. Make a sound on your head joint saying 'too' at the start. Now blow for a longer time saying 'tootootootoo'.

Experiment with tonguing different rhythms.
With the help of your teacher write your own 4 bar rhythm patterns using crotchets, minims and semibreves.

Mary had a Little Lamb

Listen to your teacher play Mary Had a little lamb on their headjoint.

(Keep the end uncovered for the high note, insert your right hand index finger up to the first knuckle for the middle note and to the second knuckle for the low note.)

Can you tell which are the high, middle and low notes?

Use your hands to show which notes are high, middle and low.

Can you play Mary had a little lamb?

With the help of your teacher can you write down your own head joint song?

_____
_____
_____
_____
_____
_____
_____
_____
_____

Beginning to Read Music

The stave is what music is written on.

It has 5 lines and 4 spaces.

As notes move up the lines and spaces the sound gets higher.

Listen to your teacher play Mary had a Little Lamb.

Can you write down when the music goes higher or lower?

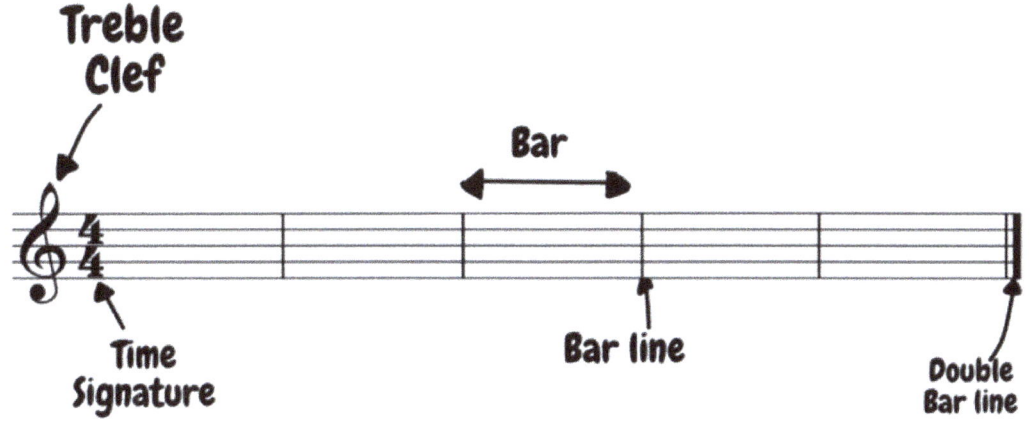

Let's get ready to Play

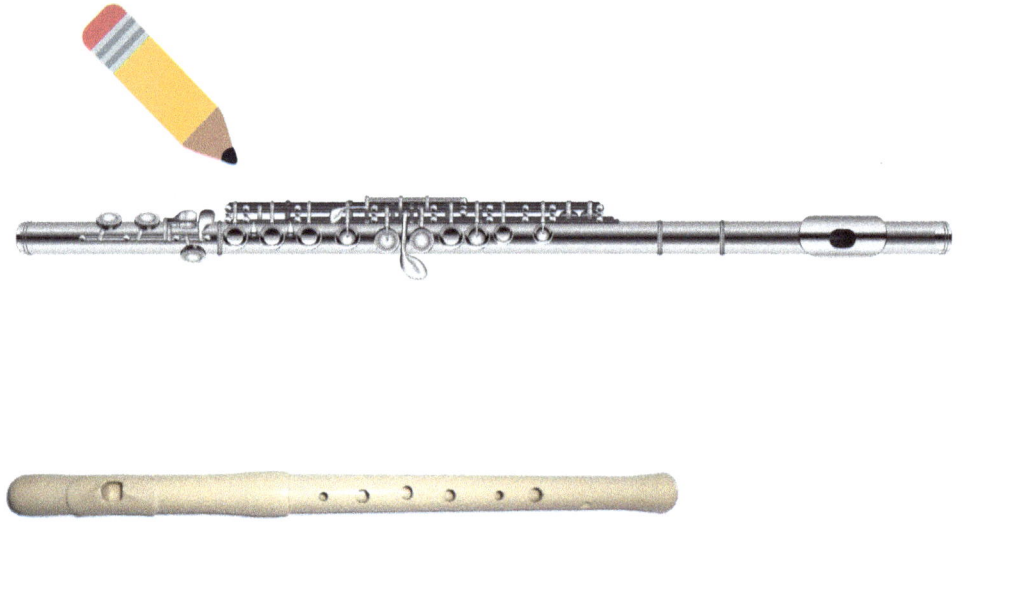

Parts of the Flute

Flutes can come in different shapes and sizes. What does your flute look like?

Does it have a curved or straight head? Is it 2 or 3 parts?

How many keys does your flute have?

With the help of your teacher label the different parts of the flute.

Putting the Flute Together

1. On a flat surface make sure that your flute case is the right way up. You can put a sticker on the right side if it is difficult to tell.

2. Take out the head joint of your flute first, making sure you are holding the smooth part not the embouchure hole.

3. Take out the body of your flute holding the smooth part at the top, not the keys. The keys of your flute are very delicate and should not be touched unless you are playing.

4. Line up the embouchure hole with the keys on the body.

5. Take out the foot joint of your flute holding the smooth part at the bottom and line up the rod of the foot joint with the keys on the body of your flute.

Flutes of different shapes and sizes must be put together in different ways.

What does your flute look like?

With your teachers help practice putting your flute together and taking it apart.

Holding your Flute

Resting your flute on your shoulder look down at the keys.
Your left hand goes on the left side of the flute and your right hand on the right side.
Looking at your hands, palms facing upwards, label your fingers 12345.

Using stickers on the keys can help you remember.

Posture when playing

Stand with your feet a shoulder width apart.

Place your left foot at 12 o'clock and your right foot in the 2 o'clock position.

Keep your shoulders down and relaxed with your chin up.

Make sure that your music stand is at eye level and your flute is parallel to your stand.

Cleaning your Flute

You should take your flute apart the same way that you put it together.

You should always clean your flute with your cleaning cloth and rod after playing.

Remember to only hold the smooth parts if your flute when cleaning.

16

 Colour me in.

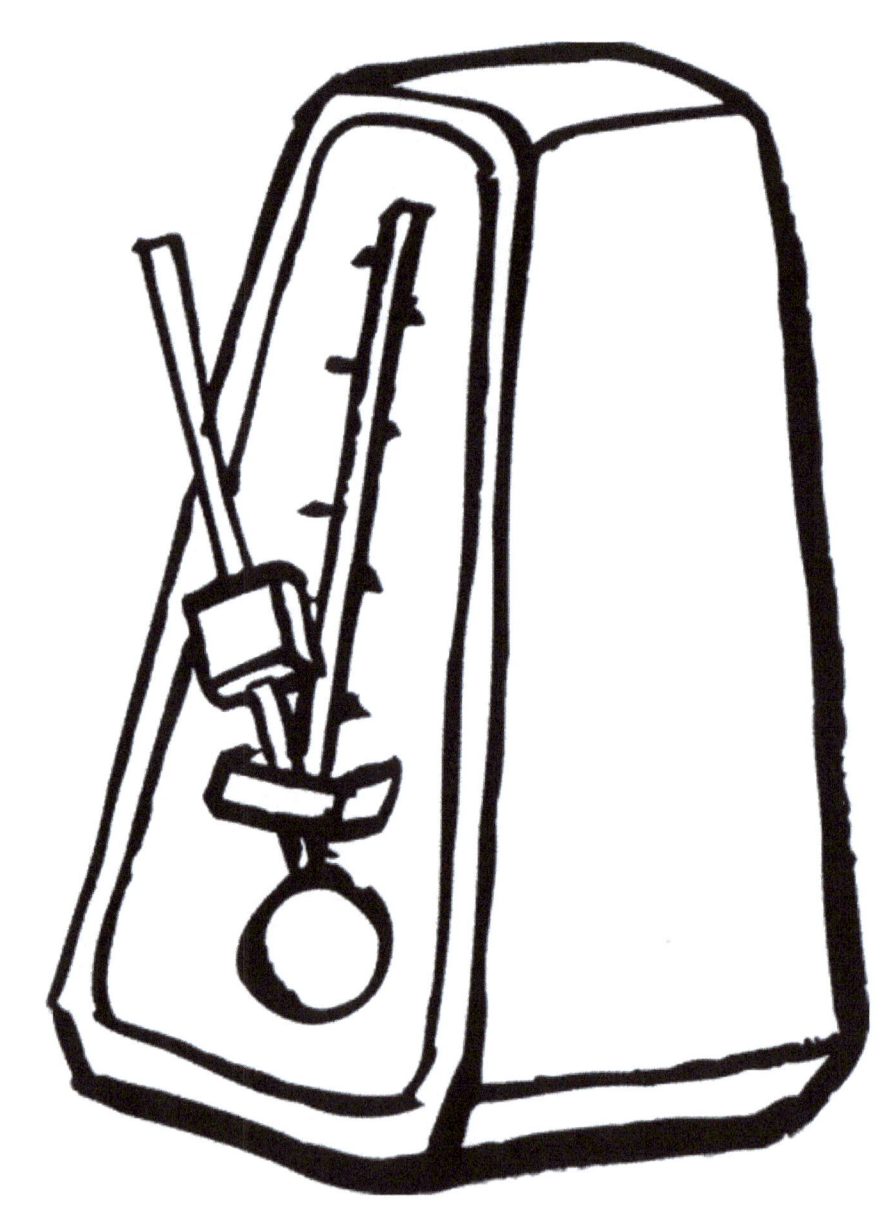

New note B/Ti

Listen to your teacher play this song.

Can you tap the beat at the same time?

- On the first beat tap your head.
- On the second beat tap your shoulders.
- On the third beat tap your knees.
- On the fourth beat tap your toes.

AS

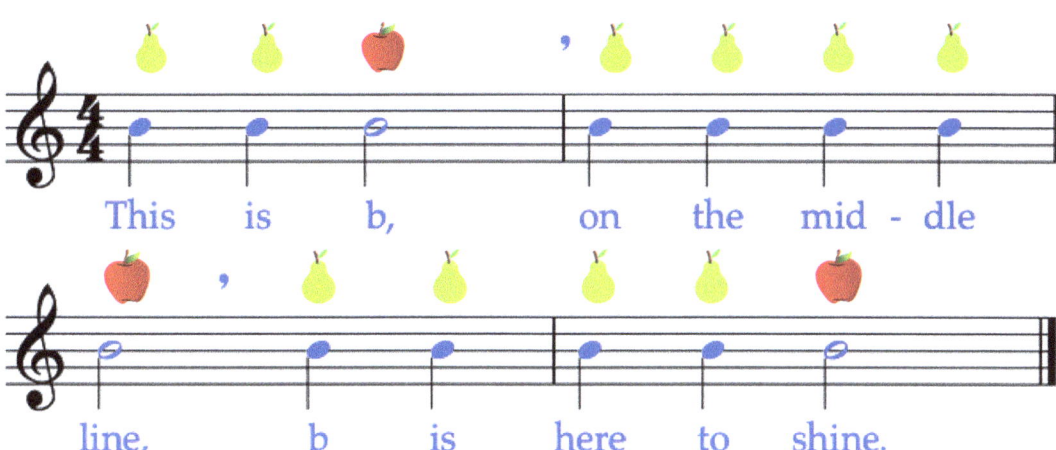

Keeping a steady pulse, copy the rhythm your teachers plays on the note B.

Now let your teacher copy you.

Remember to say 'too' at the beginning of each note.

Breath marks tell you when to take a breath. Try to only breath where the breath marks (') are.

AS

New note A/La

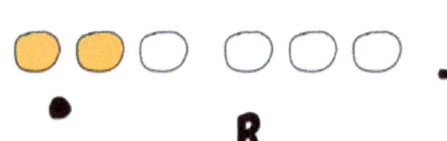

Listen to your teacher play this song.

Can you tap the beat at the same time?

- On the first beat tap your head.
- On the second beat tap your shoulders.
- On the third beat tap your knees.
- On the fourth beat tap your toes.

Keeping a steady pulse, copy the rhythm your teacher plays on the note A.
Now let your teacher copy you.

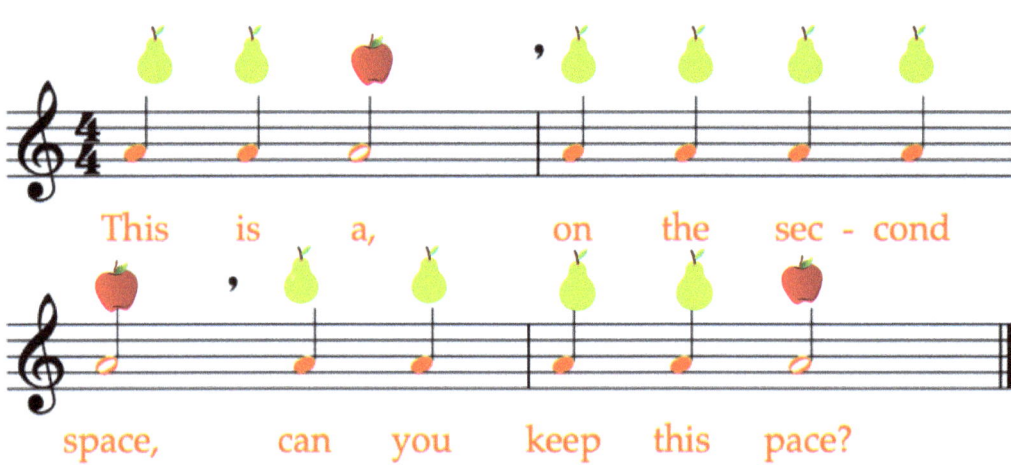

Keeping a steady pulse, practise changing between the notes B and A in this song.

Apple Song

Keeping a steady pulse, clap the rhythm of this song.
Try to only breathe where the breath marks are.

AS

I Love to Play Music

Keeping a steady pulse, clap the rhythm of this song.
Try to only breathe where the breath marks are.

AS

Can you play this off by heart?

New note G/Sol

Listen to your teacher play this song.

Can you tap the beat at the same time?

- On the first beat tap your head.
- On the second beat tap your shoulders.
- On the third beat tap your knees.
- On the fourth beat tap your toes.

Keeping a steady pulse, copy the rhythm your teacher plays on the note G. Now let your teacher copy you.

Remember to say 'too' at the beginning of each note.

Keeping a steady pulse, practise changing between the notes B, A and G.

Hello, How Are You?

Keeping a steady pulse, clap the rhythm of this song.

Remember to only breathe where the breath marks are.

AS

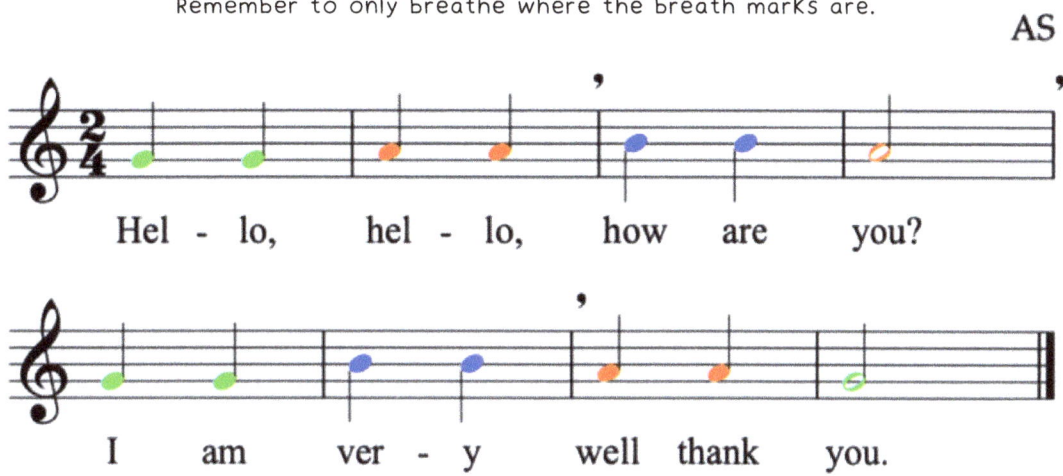

I Love to Play

Keeping a steady pulse, clap the rhythm of this song.

Remember to only breathe where the breath marks are.

AS

With the help of your teacher write out the counting above the notes.

Remember to only breathe where the breath marks are.

Can you remember their names?

 Colour me in.

Dynamics

Forte or *f* means loud.

To play loudly take a big breath and blow strongly.

Piano or *p* means quiet.

To play quietly squeeze from your tummy muscles and blow softly.

Practice playing forte and piano in these songs.

Do you recognise these tunes?

Remember to say 'too' at the beginning of each note.

Rests

Rests are a sign that tell you to be silent.

This is a crotchet rest.   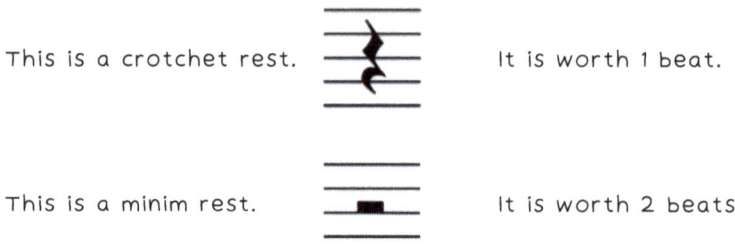   It is worth 1 beat.

This is a minim rest.   It is worth 2 beats.

First say, then clap the rhythm.

You can say 'sh' on the rests to help you count.

AS

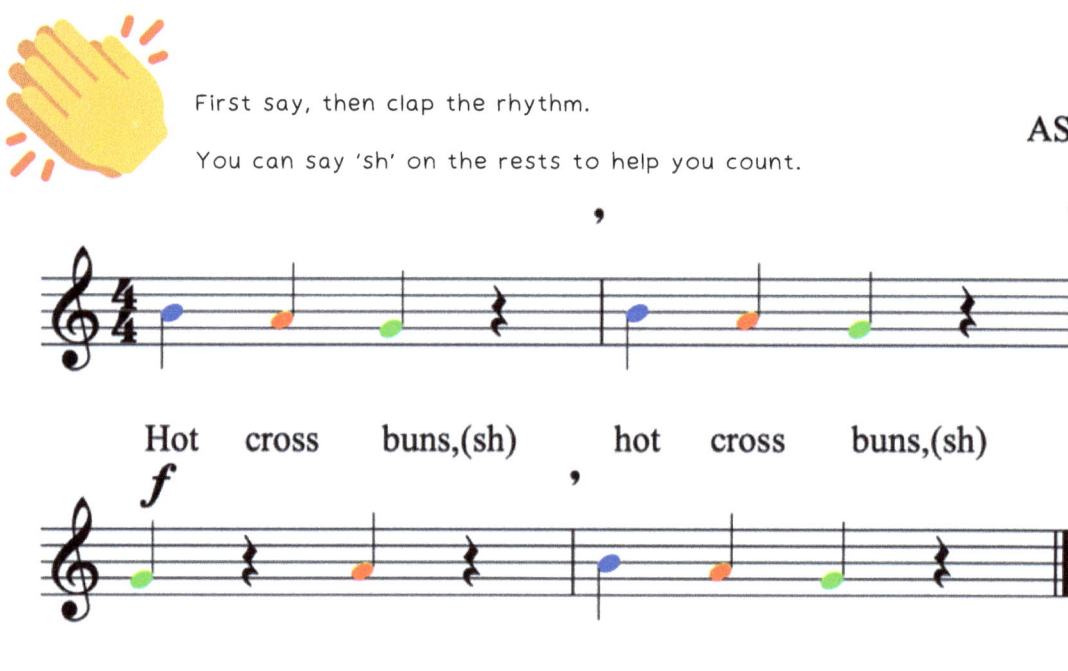

Hot cross buns,(sh)   hot cross buns,(sh)

hot,(sh)   cross,(sh)   hot cross buns.(sh)

With the help of your teacher write the counting out above the stave.

AS

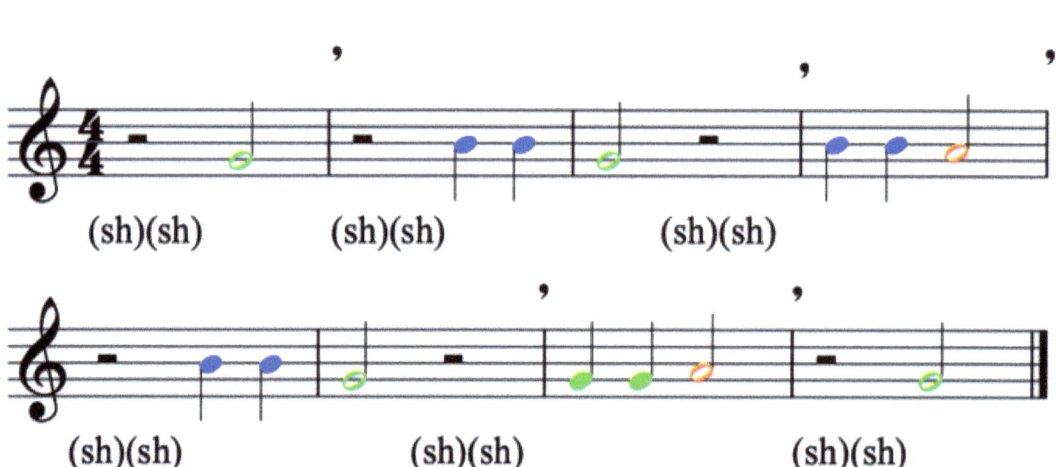

(sh)(sh)   (sh)(sh)   (sh)(sh)

(sh)(sh)   (sh)(sh)   (sh)(sh)

Dynamics Song

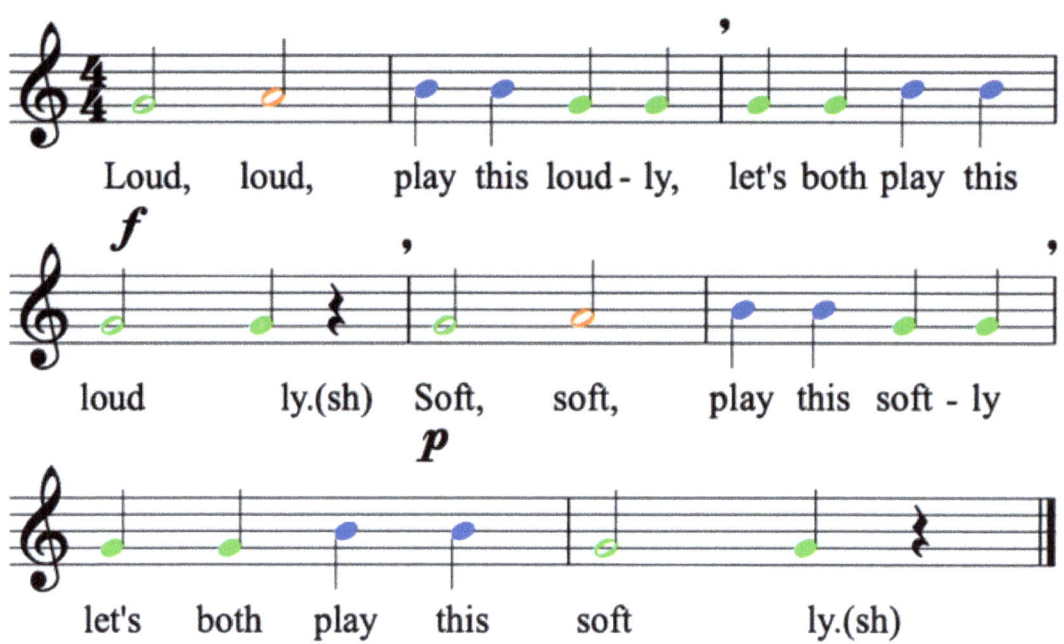

 Colour me in.

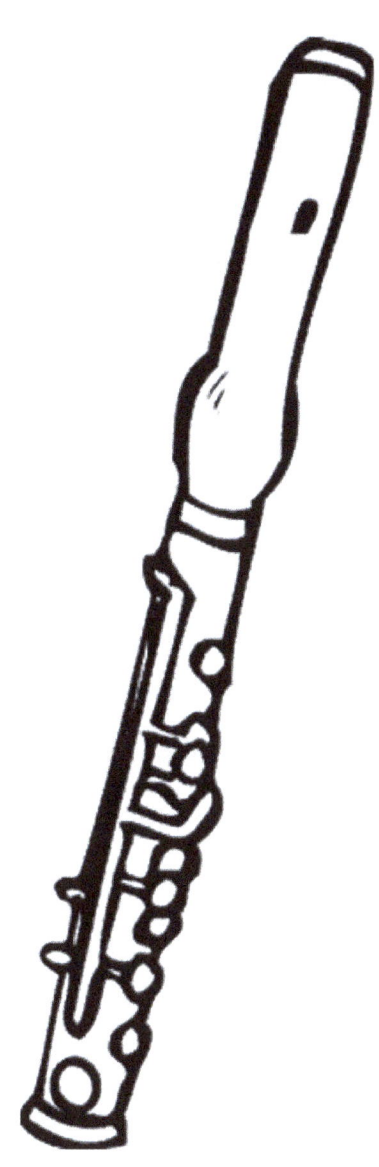

New note C /Do'

Listen to your teacher play this song.

Can you tap the beat at the same time?

- On the first beat tap your head.
- On the second beat tap your shoulders.
- On the third beat tap your Knees.
- On the fourth beat tap your toes.

Keeping a steady pulse, copy the rhythm your teacher plays on the note C.

Now let your teacher copy you.

Practice balancing your flute on your chin, your right-hand thumb and your left-hand pointing finger.

Remember to say 'too' at the beginning of each note.

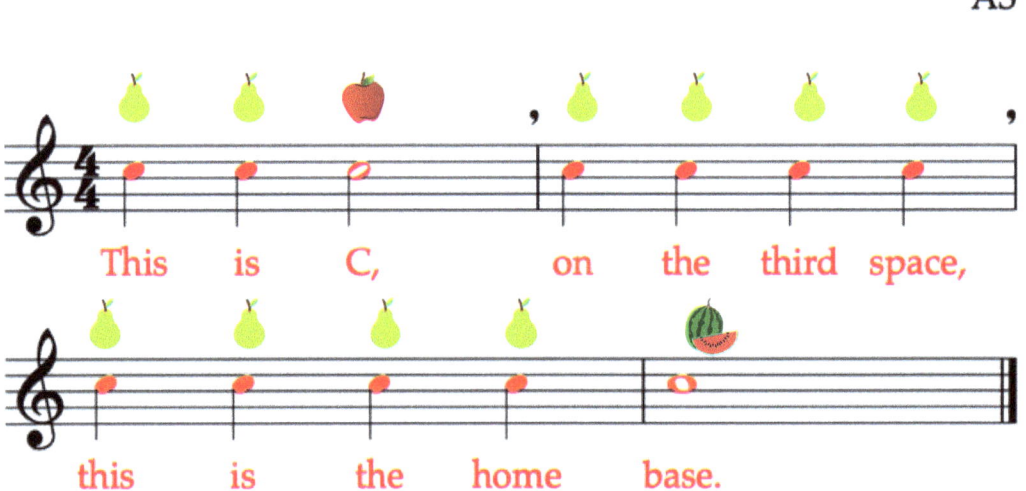

How quickly can you change between B and C?

Practice playing 'BCBCBCBCBC' as fast as you can.

Try to Keep your flute still.

Keeping a steady pulse, practise changing between the notes C, B, A and G in these exercises.

Watch out for dynamic changes in these exercises.

AS

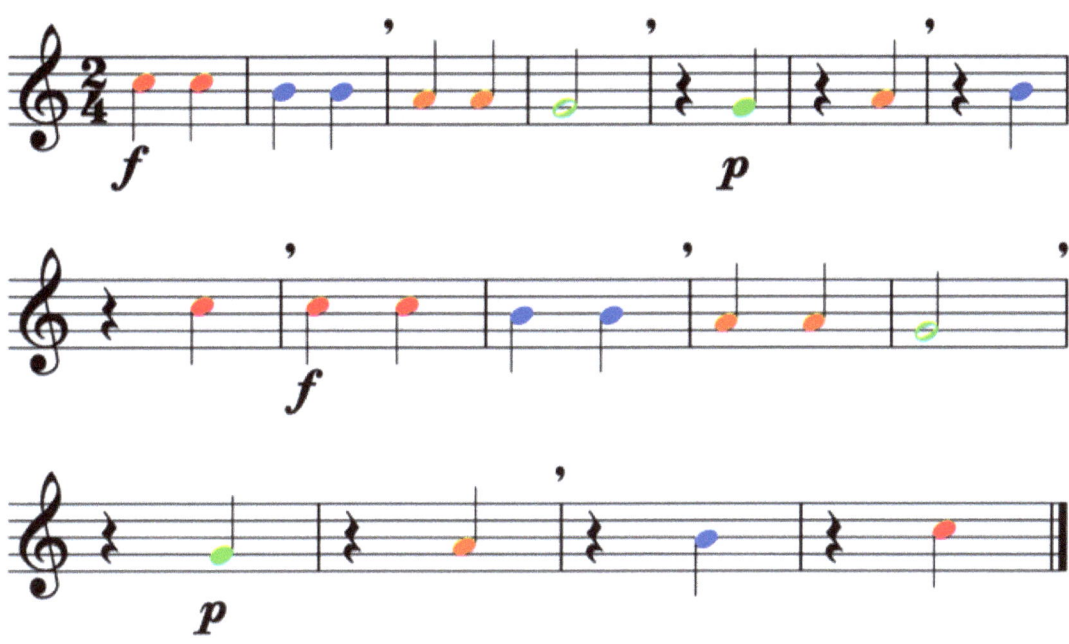

AS

Not too Fast, Not too Slow

AS

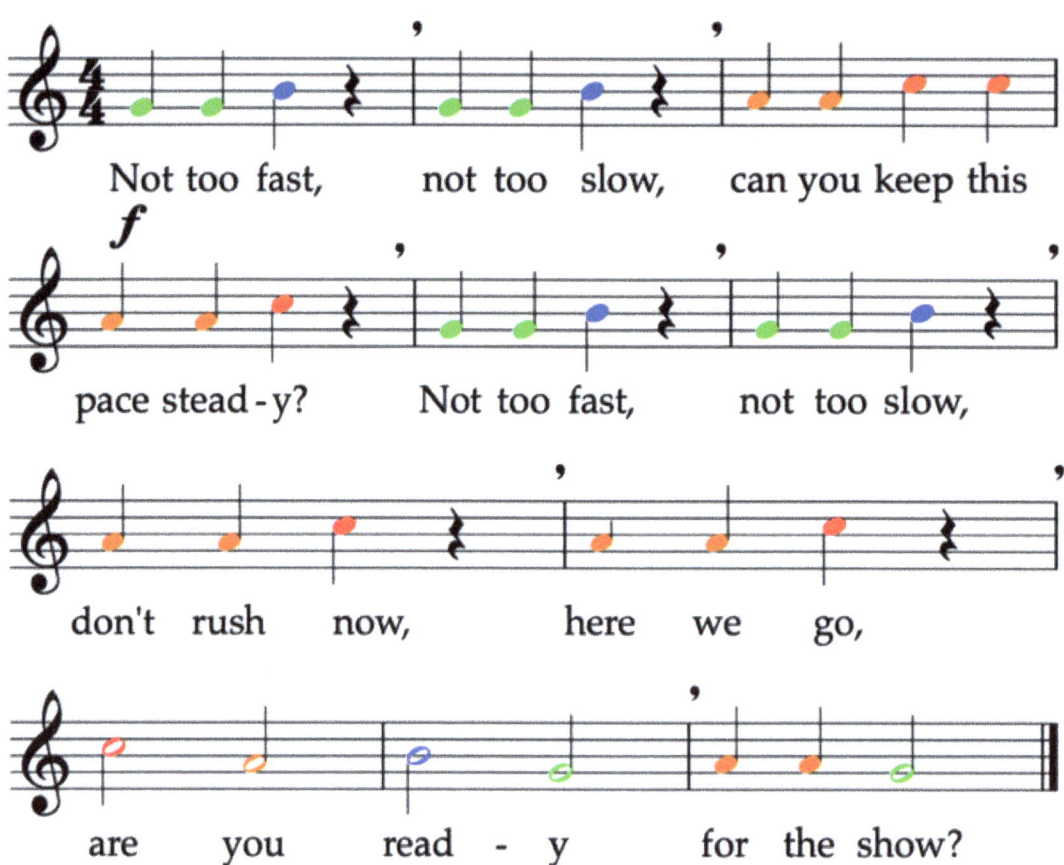

3/4 This means that there are 3 crotchet beats in a bar.

Say, then clap these rhythms.

Do they feel different to 2/4 and 4/4? How so?

AS

Now play these rhythms on your flute.

Remember to say 'too' at the beginning of each note.

AS

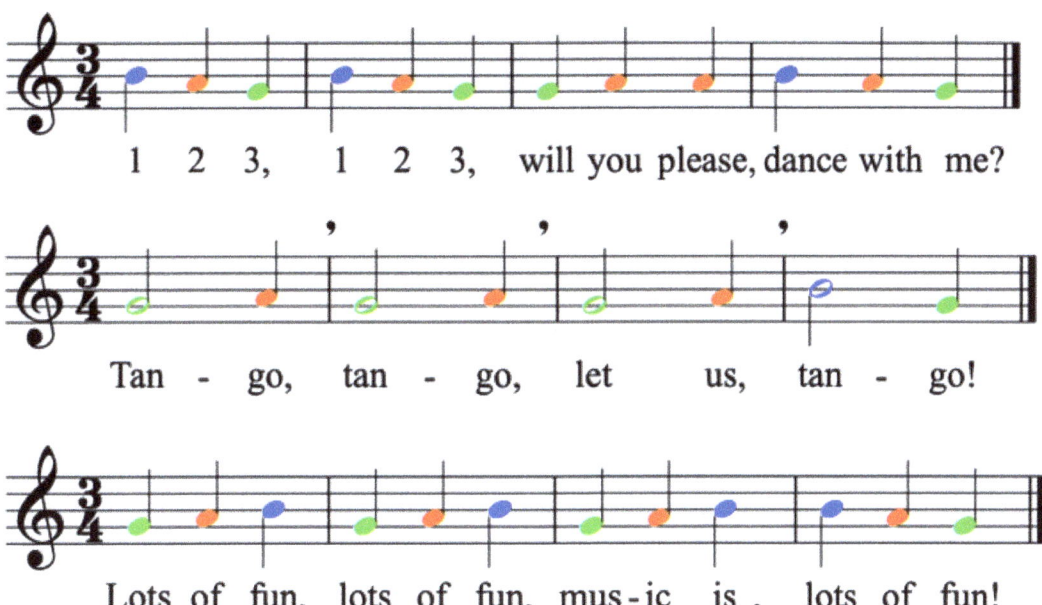

1 2 3,   1 2 3,   will you please, dance with me?

Tan - go, tan - go, let us, tan - go!

Lots of fun, lots of fun, mus-ic is, lots of fun!

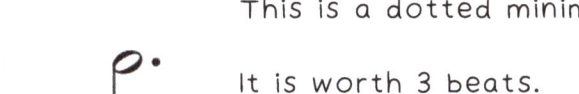

This is a dotted minim.

It is worth 3 beats.

It sounds like BA-NA-NA.

Banana Song

Say, then clap the rhythm in this song.

AS

Banana,   banana,   banana   1, 2, 3,

f

1, 2, 3, banana, banana banana.

Jack and Jill

trd arr. AS

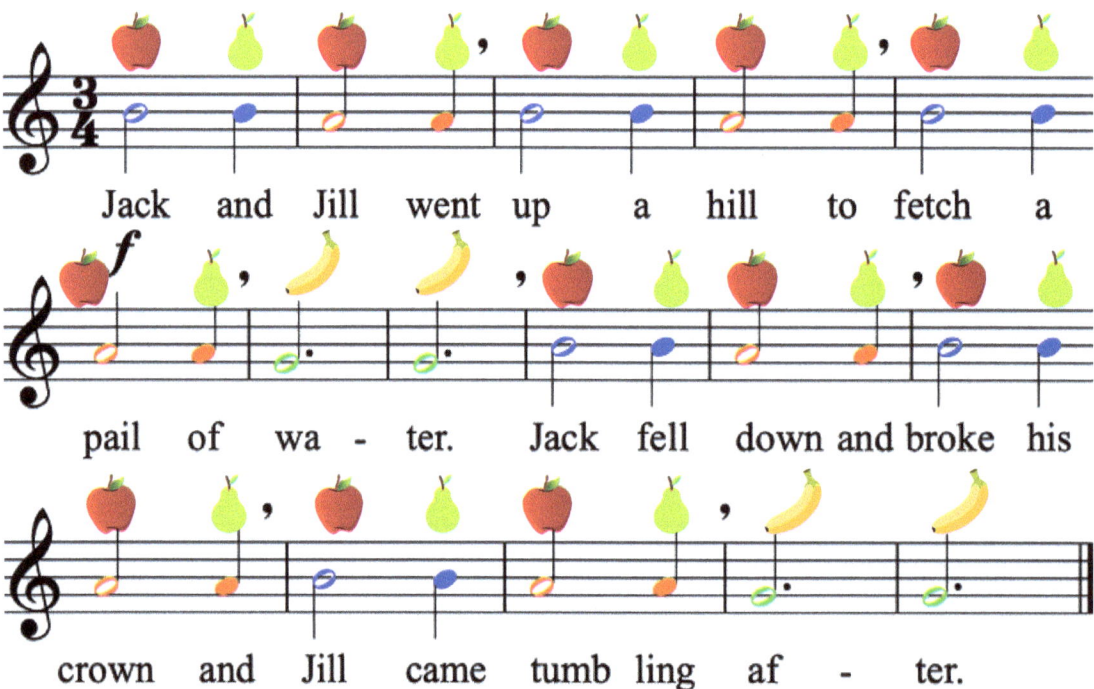

Jack and Jill went up a hill to fetch a pail of wa-ter. Jack fell down and broke his crown and Jill came tumb ling af - ter.

 Colour me in.

Articulation

Slurs are curved lines over or under notes. These tell you to only tongue the first note. You should play this is in one big breath.

Now practice tonguing and slurring in these exercises.

Keeping a steady pulse first clap the rhythm.

Then sing with your teacher saying 'too'.

AS

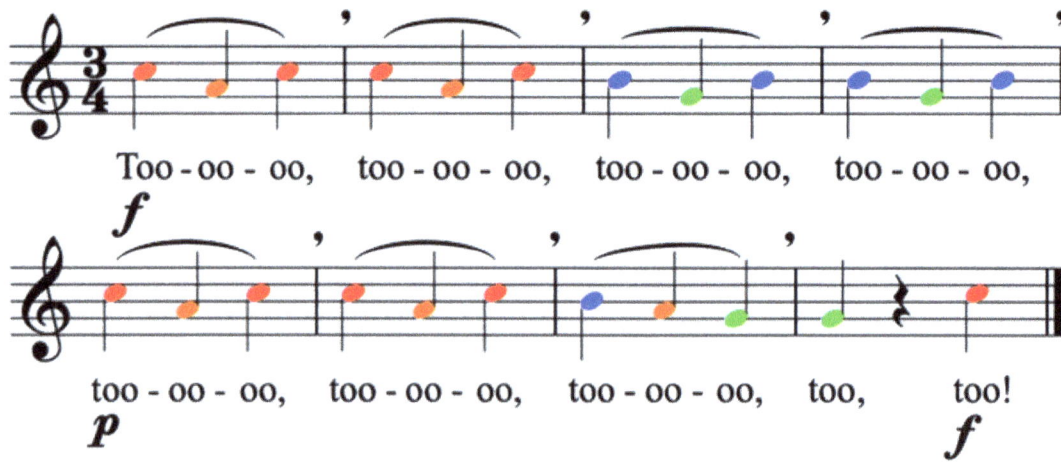

Too - oo - oo,   too - oo - oo,   too - oo - oo,   too - oo - oo,
too - oo - oo,   too - oo - oo,   too - oo - oo,   too,   too!

With the help of your teacher write out above the stave where you should be tonguing.

Remember to only breathe where the breath marks are.

AS

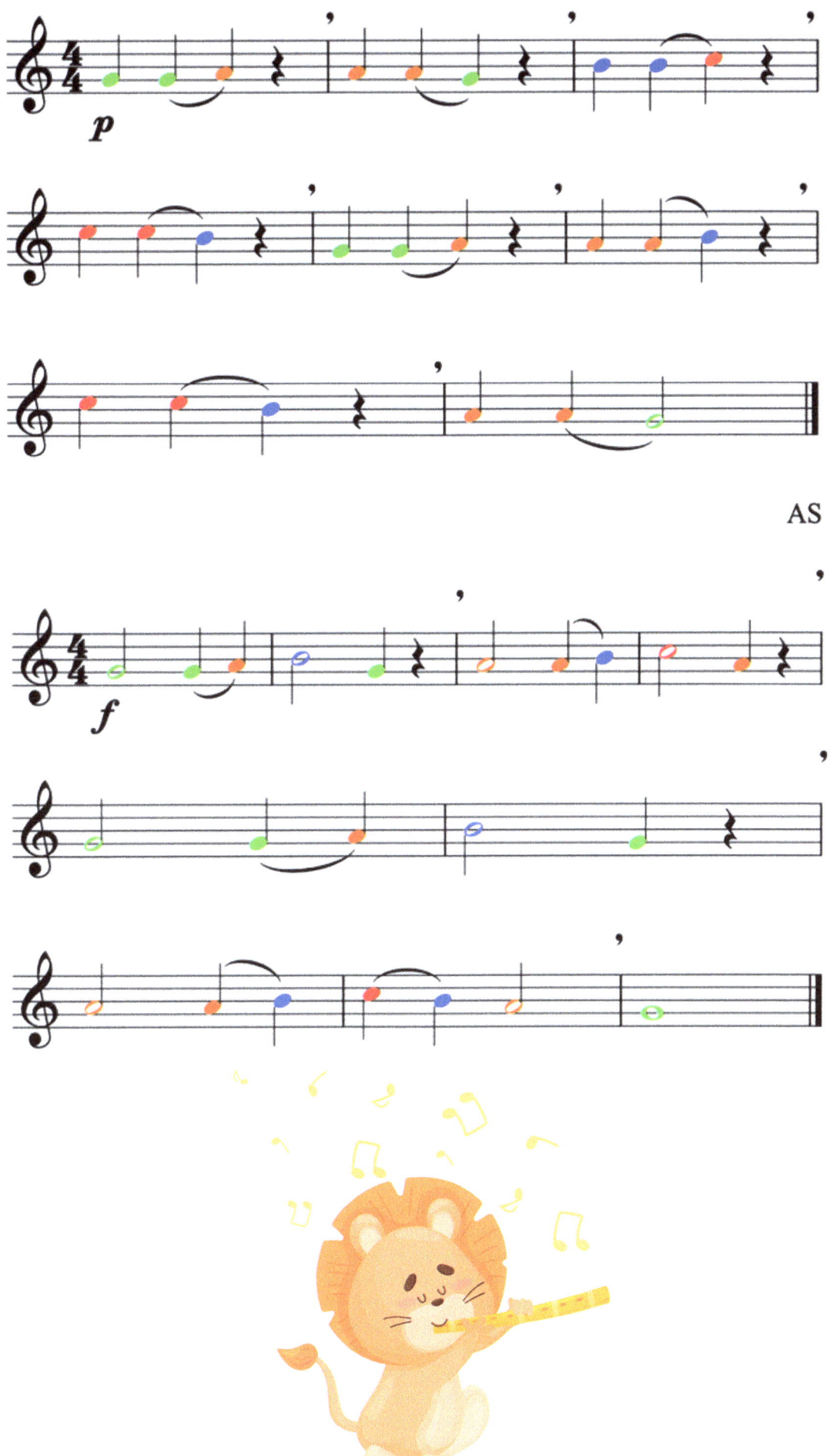

Staccato

Staccato notes are short and detached.

They sound like hiccups!

These are marked with a dot underneath or on top of the note head.

First say, then play this piece.

Remember to keep your tonguing light and bouncy.

AS

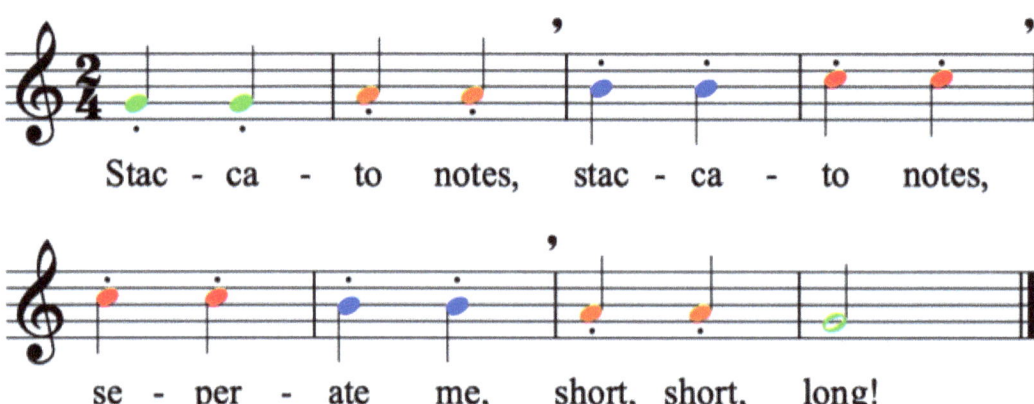

Stac - ca - to notes, stac - ca - to notes,

se - per - ate me, short, short, long!

Owl Song
Watch out for the dynamic changes in this piece.

AS

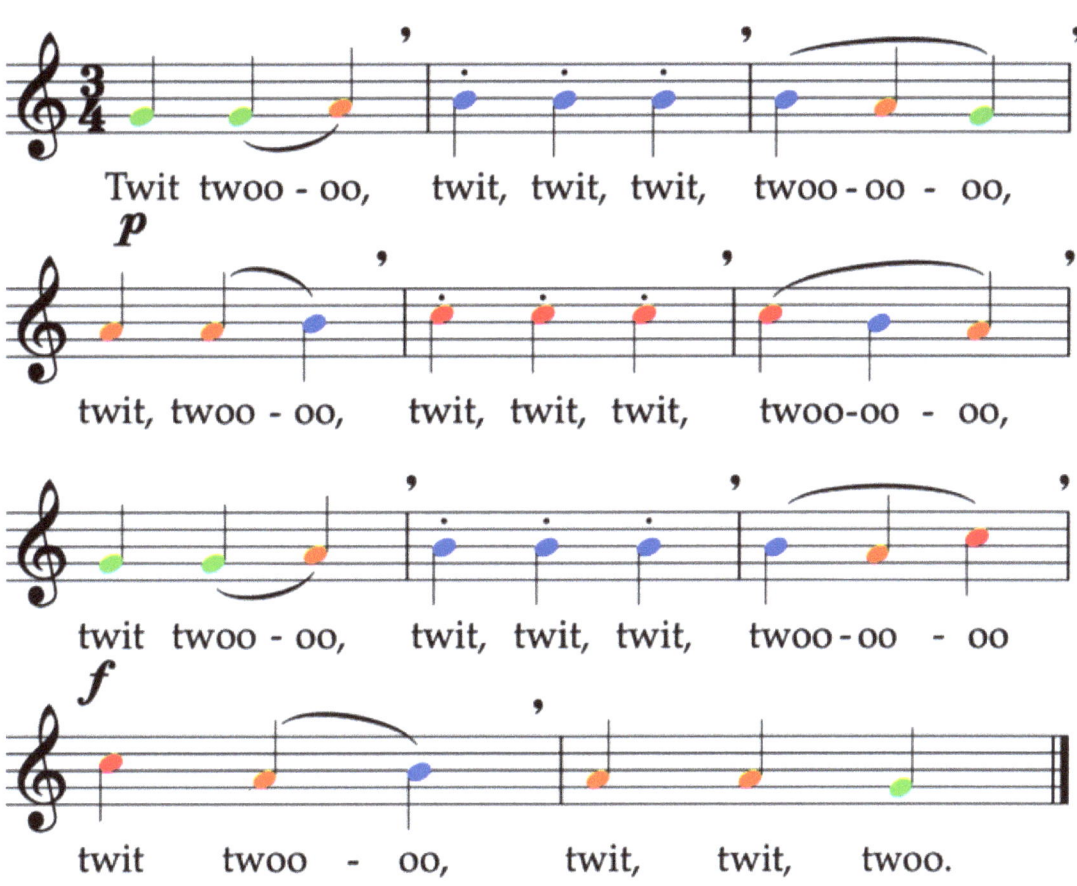

New Note F/Fa

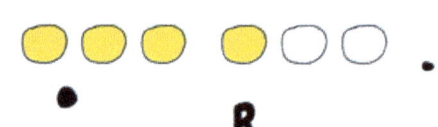

Listen to your teacher play this song.

Can you tap the beat at the same time?

- On the first beat tap your head.
- On the second beat tap your shoulders.
- On the third beat tap your knees.
- On the fourth beat tap your toes.

Keeping a steady pulse, copy the rhythm your teachers plays on the note F.

Now let your teacher copy you. **AS**

This is f, on the first space,
re - mem - ber not too race.

This a quaver beat.

When 2 quavers are next to each other it looks like this.

This sounds like CHER-RY.

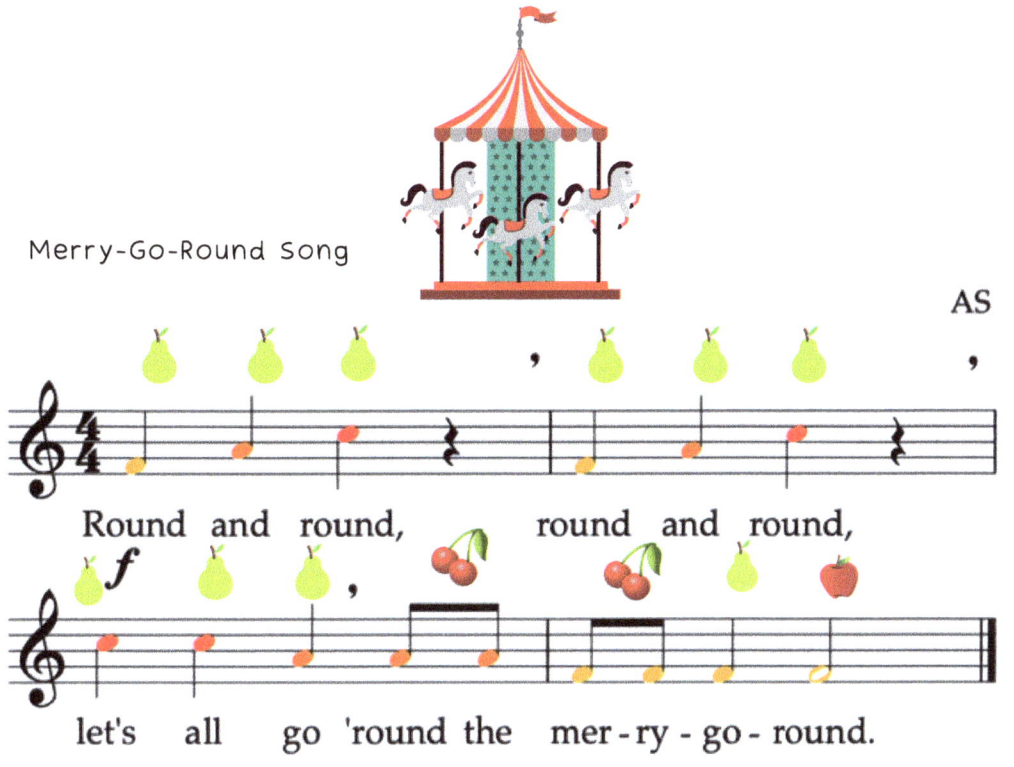

Merry-Go-Round Song

Round and round, round and round, let's all go 'round the mer-ry-go-round.

Can you play this off by heart?

Now practice these the exercises.

Keeping a steady pulse first clap the rhythm.

Can you write the counting above the notes?

Remember the dynamic markings.

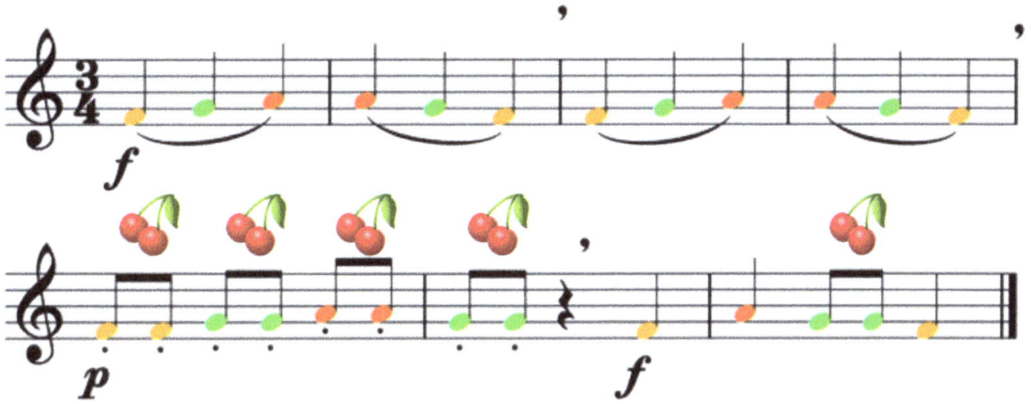

AS

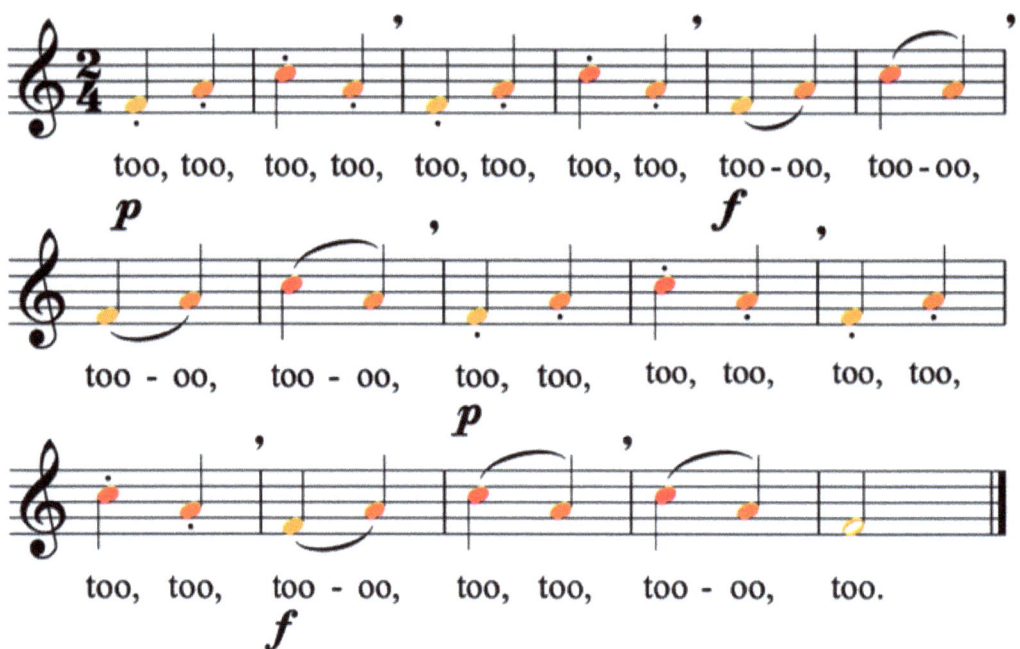

Dynamics (crescendo and decrescendo)

This sign ⟨ tells you to gradually get louder. The Italian term is crescendo.

This sign ⟩ tells you to gradually get quieter. The Italian term is decrescendo.

To get louder blow more air and push from your tummy muscles.

To get softer control the air flow and squeeze from your tummy muscles.

Long Note Gymnastics

Practice getting louder on these long notes.

Remember to tongue the beginning of each note

AS

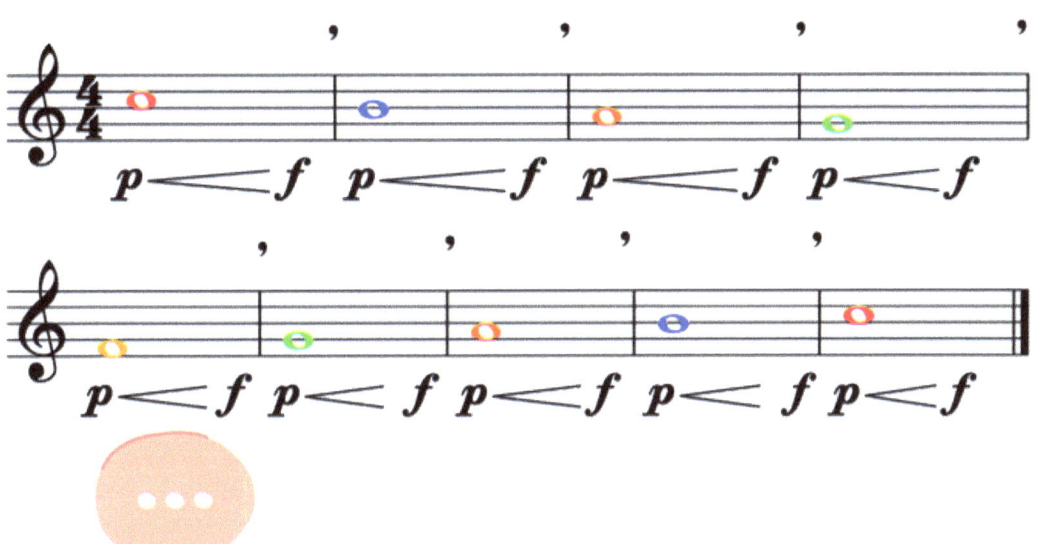

Practice getting softer on these long notes.

Remember to tongue the beginning of each note.

AS

New Note E/Mi

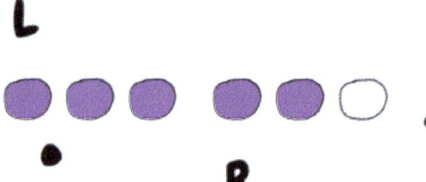

Listen to your teacher play this song.

Can you tap the beat at the same time?

- On the first beat tap your head.
- On the second beat tap your shoulders.
- On the third beat tap your Knees.
- On the fourth beat tap your toes.

Keeping a steady pulse, copy the rhythm your teacher plays on the note E.

Now let your teacher copy you.

AS

This is e, on the first line,

let's do the grape vine!

New Note D/Re

Listen to your teacher play this song.

Can you tap the beat at the same time?

- On the first beat tap your head.
- On the second beat tap your shoulders.
- On the third beat tap your knees.
- On the fourth beat tap your toes.

Keeping a steady pulse, copy the rhythm your teacher plays on the note D.

Now let your teacher copy you.

AS

This is d, be-low the first line, she is on cloud nine!

AS

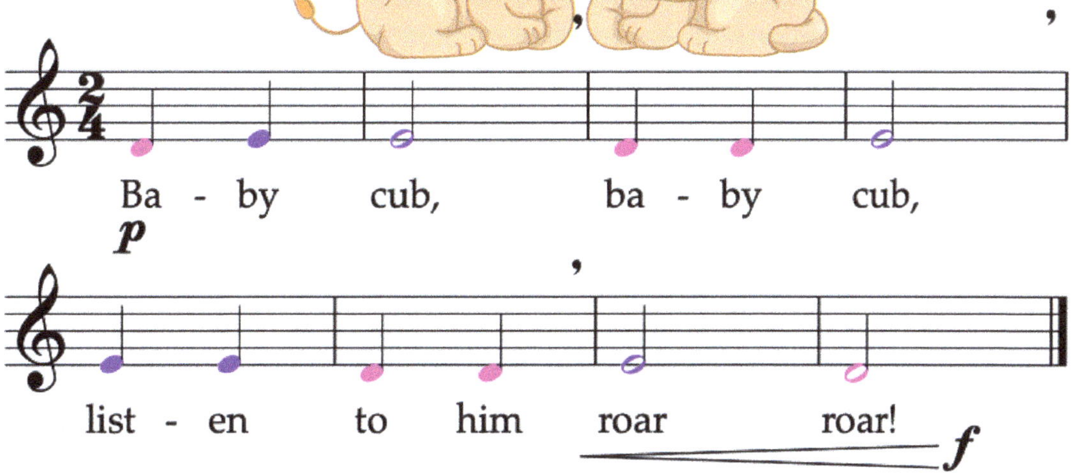

Ba - by cub, ba - by cub, list - en to him roar roar!

p .... *f*

 Colour me in.

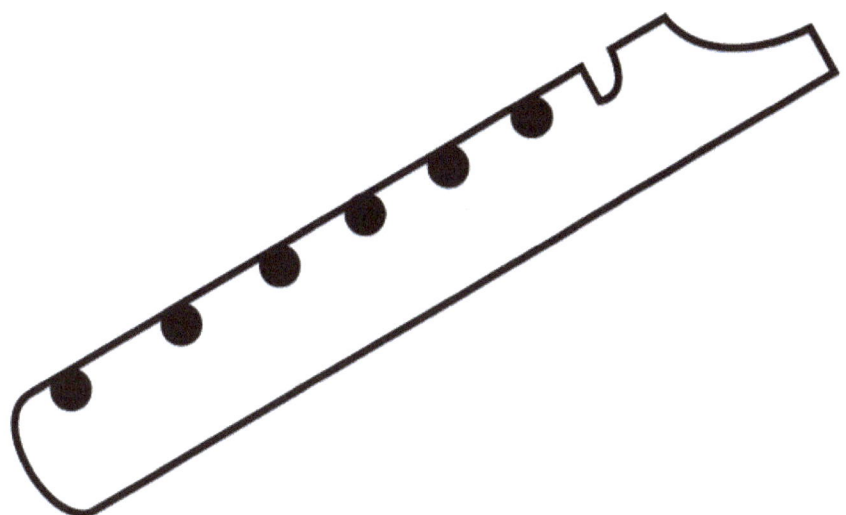

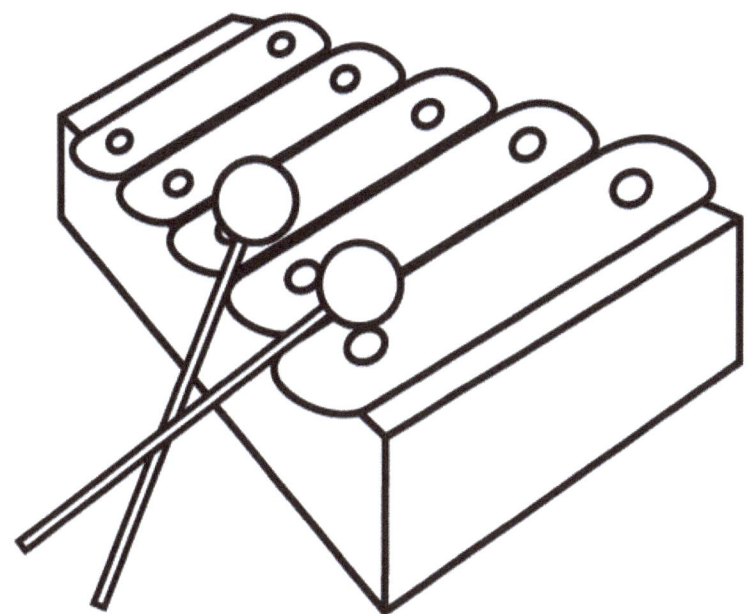

New Note Low C/Do

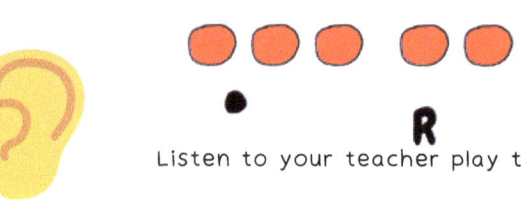

Listen to your teacher play this song.

Can you tap the beat at the same time?

- On the first beat tap your head.
- On the second beat tap your shoulders.
- On the third beat tap your knees.
- On the fourth beat tap your toes.

Keeping a steady pulse, copy the rhythm your teacher plays on the note C. **AS**

Now let your teacher copy you.

Hel - lo c how are you?

On the led-ger line feel-ing might-y fine.

C Major Scale

A scale is a pattern of notes next to each other that go up and down.

Can you learn these patterns off by heart?

Remember to only breathe where the breath marks are. **AS**

Do Re Mi Fa Sol La Ti Do'

Do' Ti La Sol Fa Mi Re Do

C major Arpeggio

An arpeggio is a pattern of notes that uses the 1st, 3rd and 5th note of a scale.

Can you learn these patterns off by heart?

Remember to only breathe where the breath marks are.

Now practice these songs which use the note low C.

Do you recognise these tunes?

The Farmer in the Dell

trd arr. AS

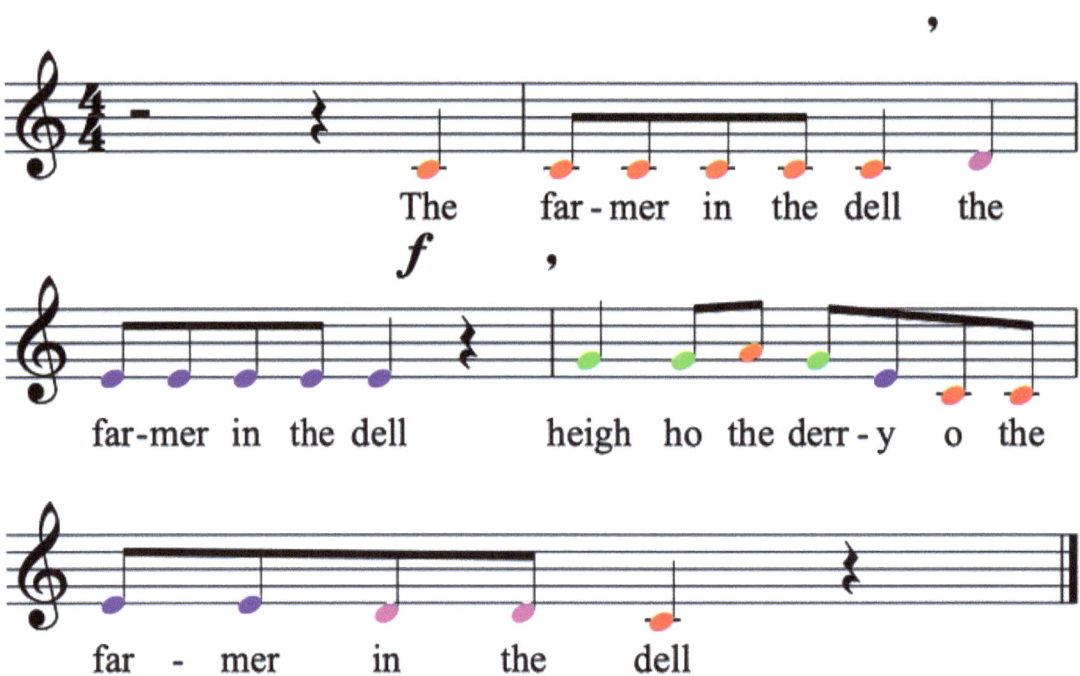

ABC Song

trd arr. AS

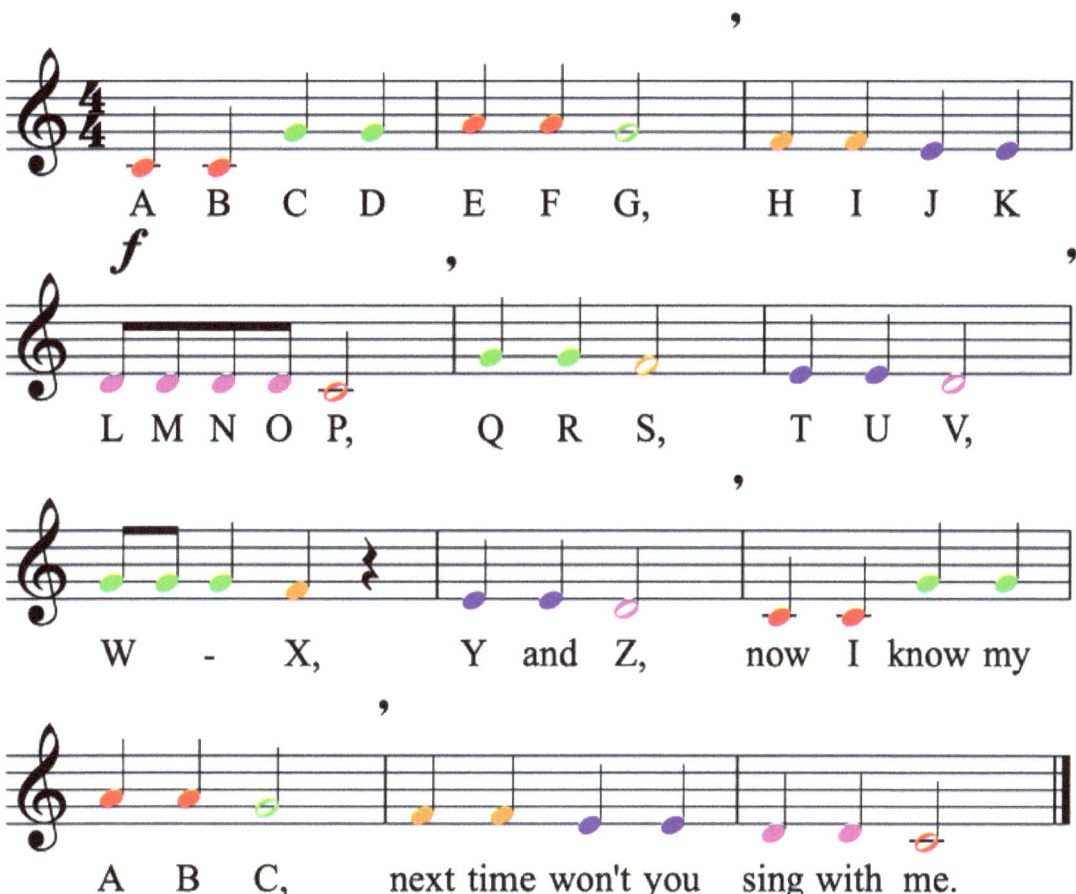

Are you sleeping?

trd arr. AS

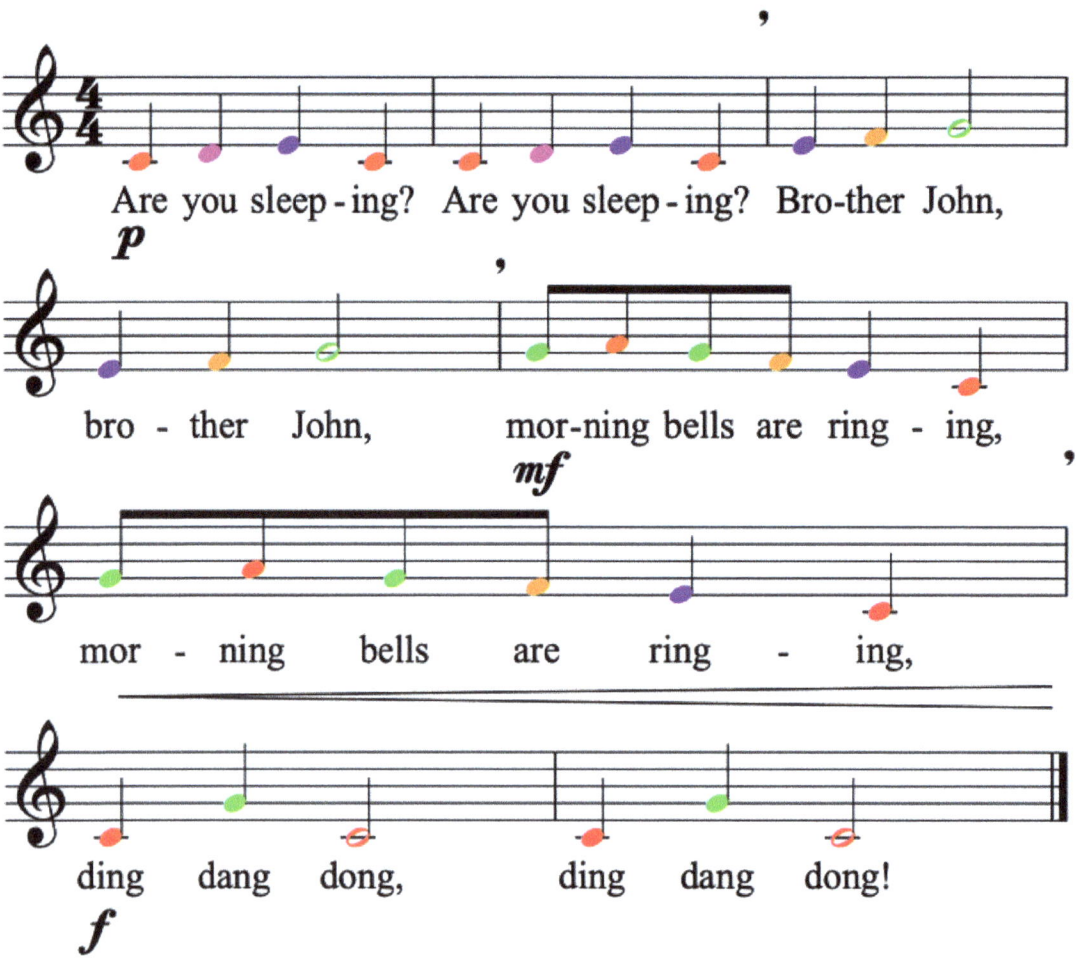

Hot Cross Buns

trd arr. AS

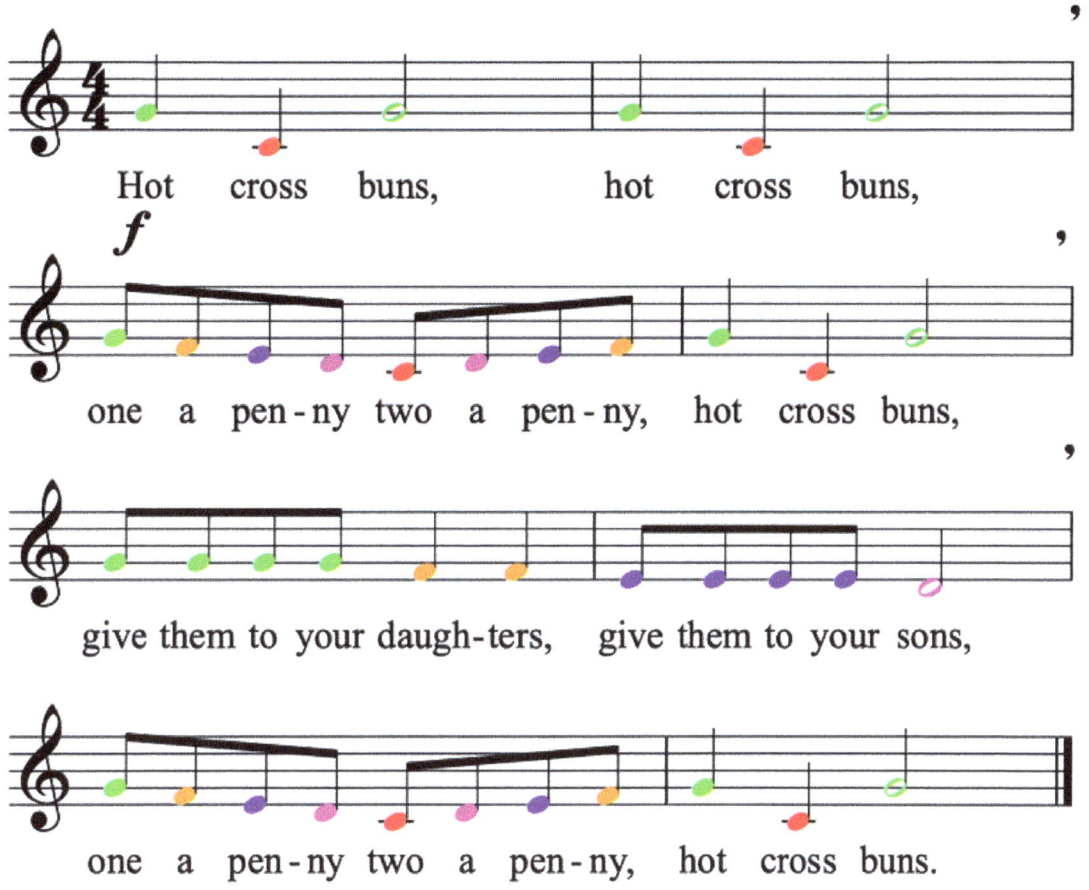

Twinkle, Twinkle Little Star

trd arr. AS

On Top of Old Smokey

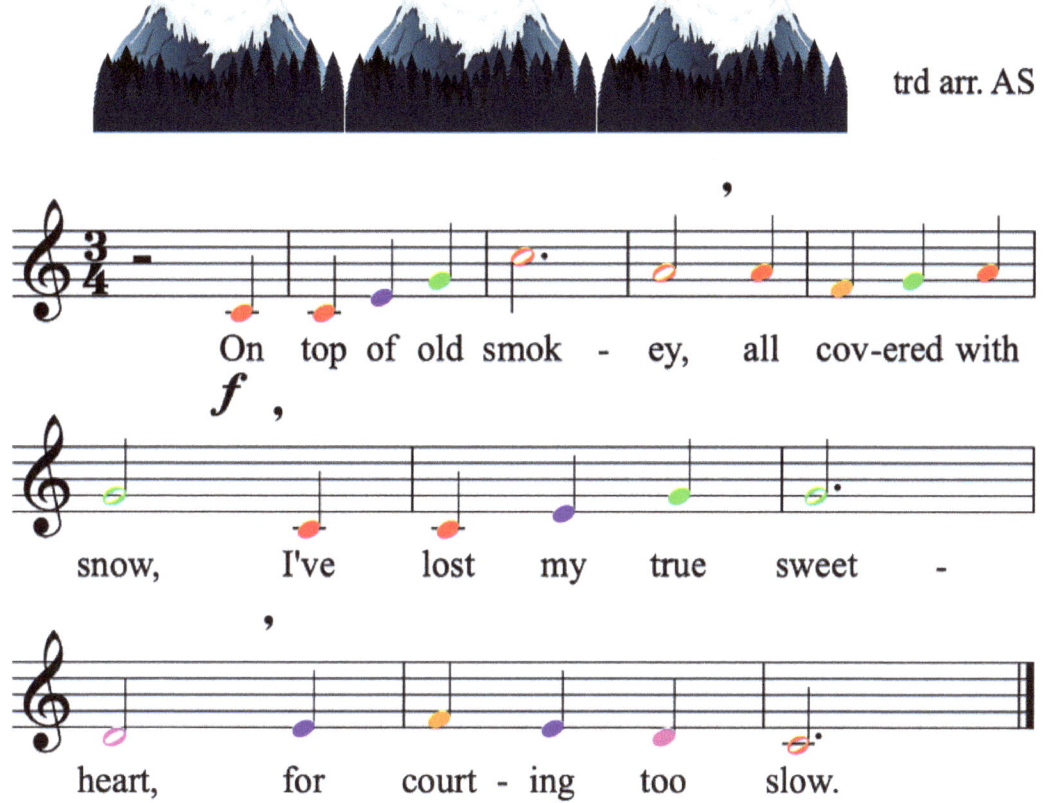

trd arr. AS

Can Can

Jacques Offenbach arr. AS

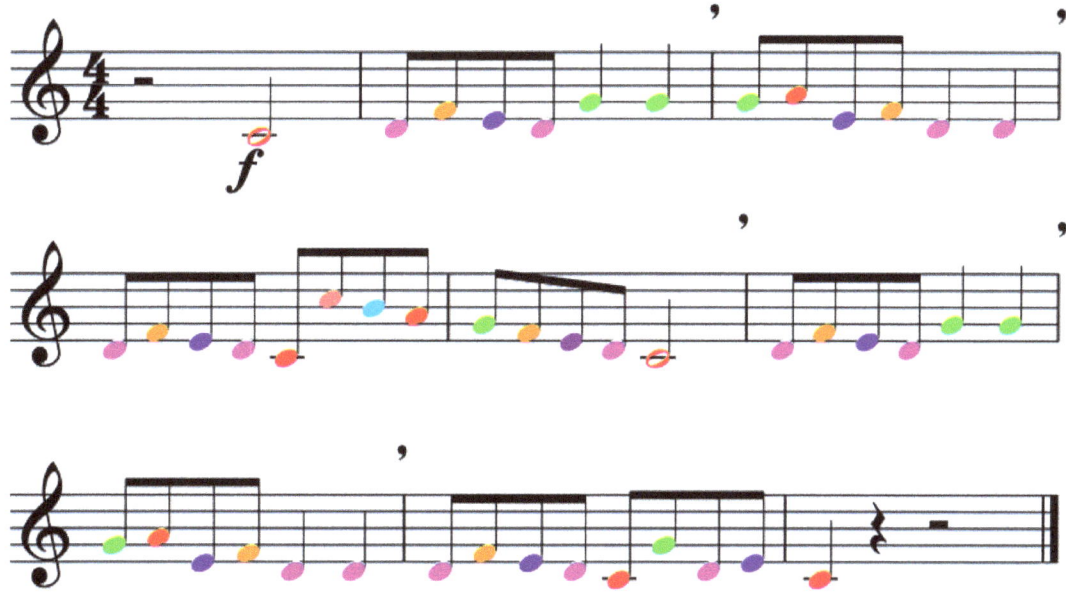

Brahms Lullaby

J.Brahms arr. AS

Baa Baa Black Sheep

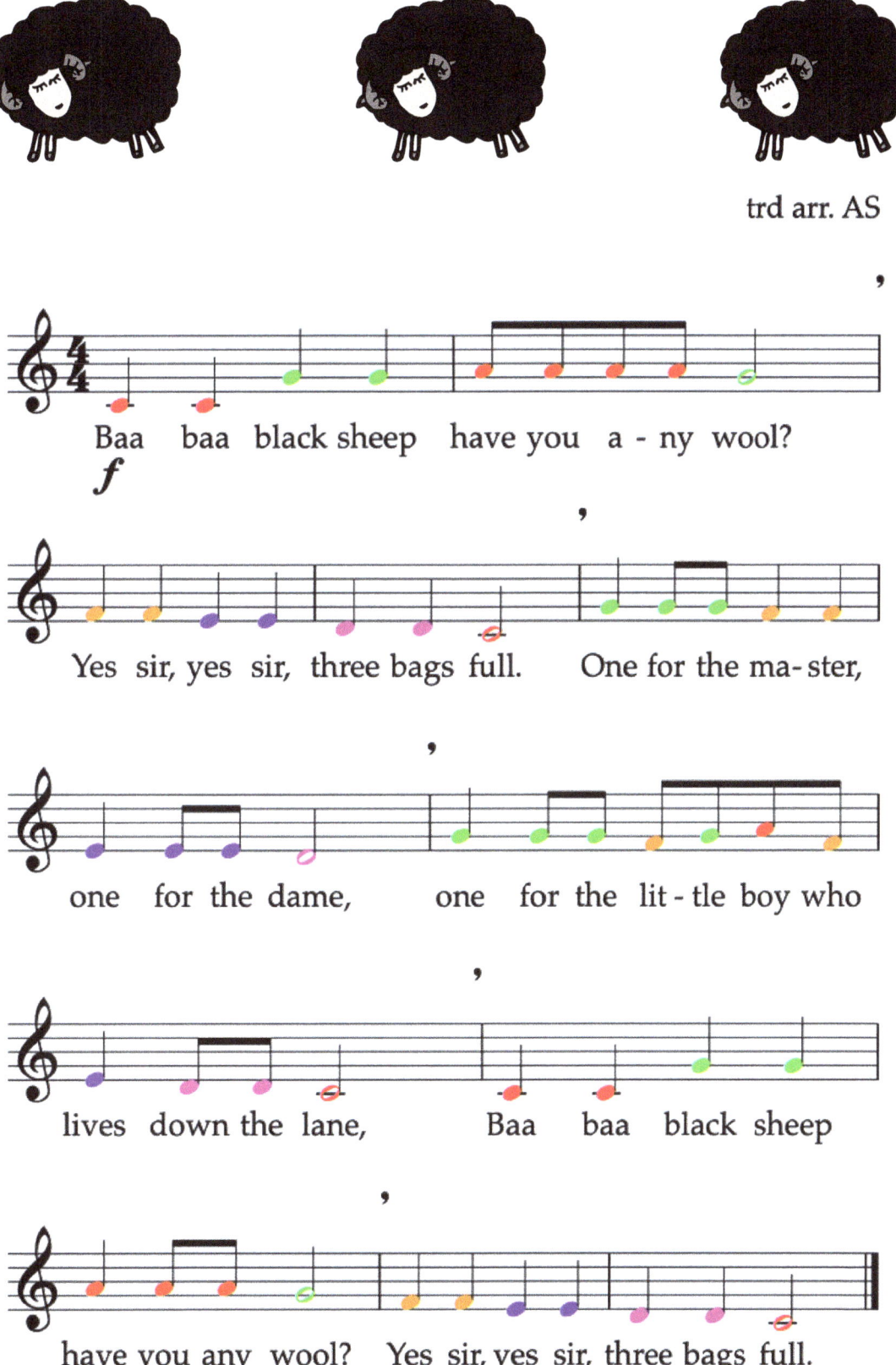

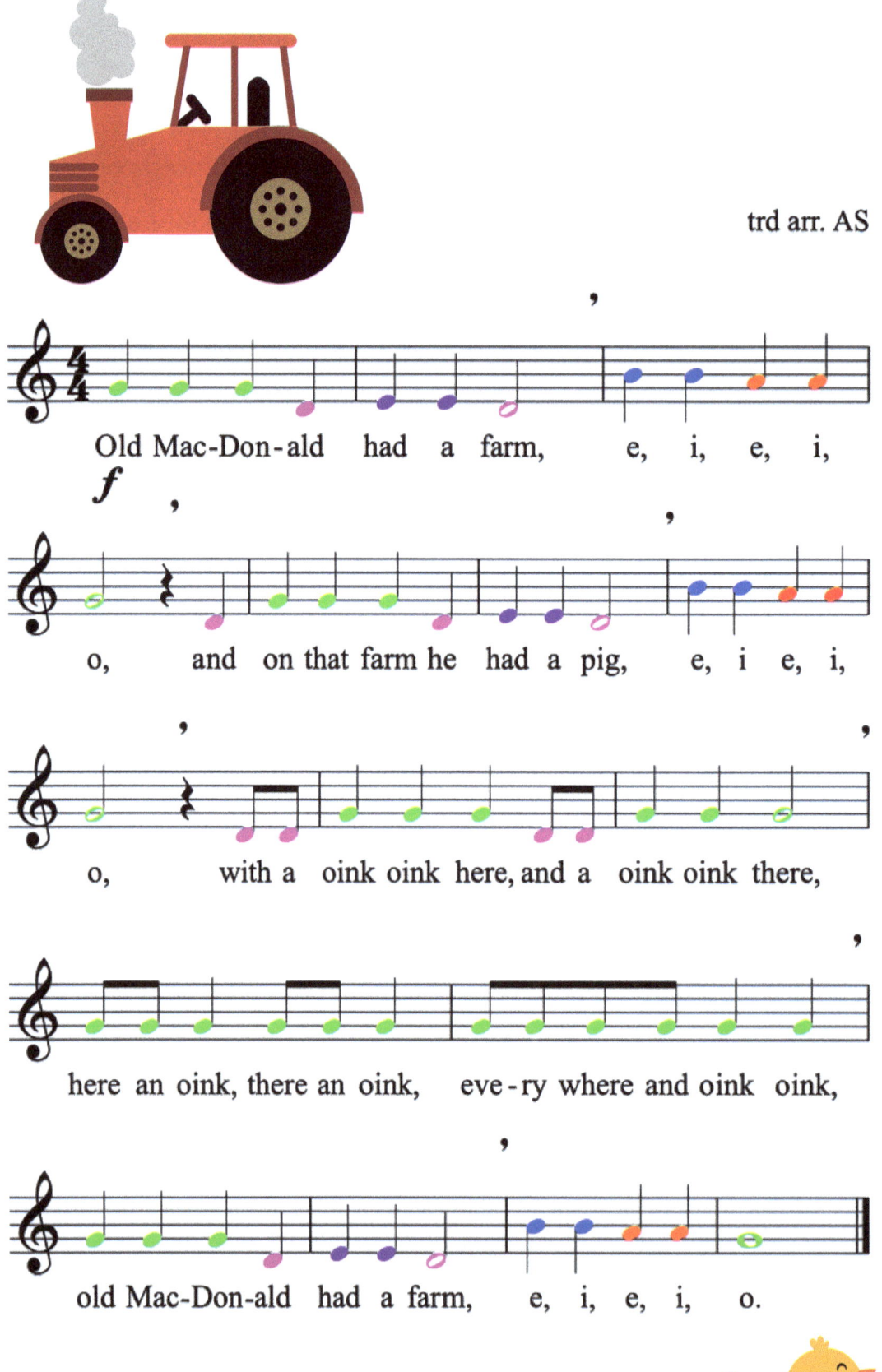

Dancing Dinosaurs

AS

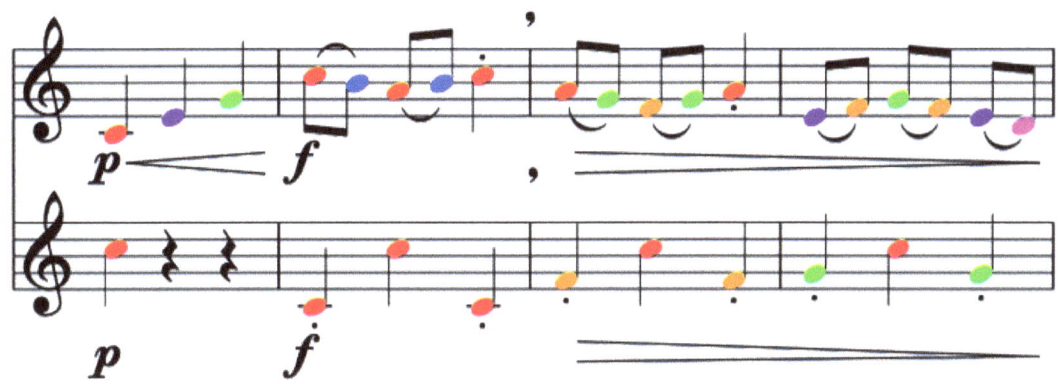

Singing Sailor

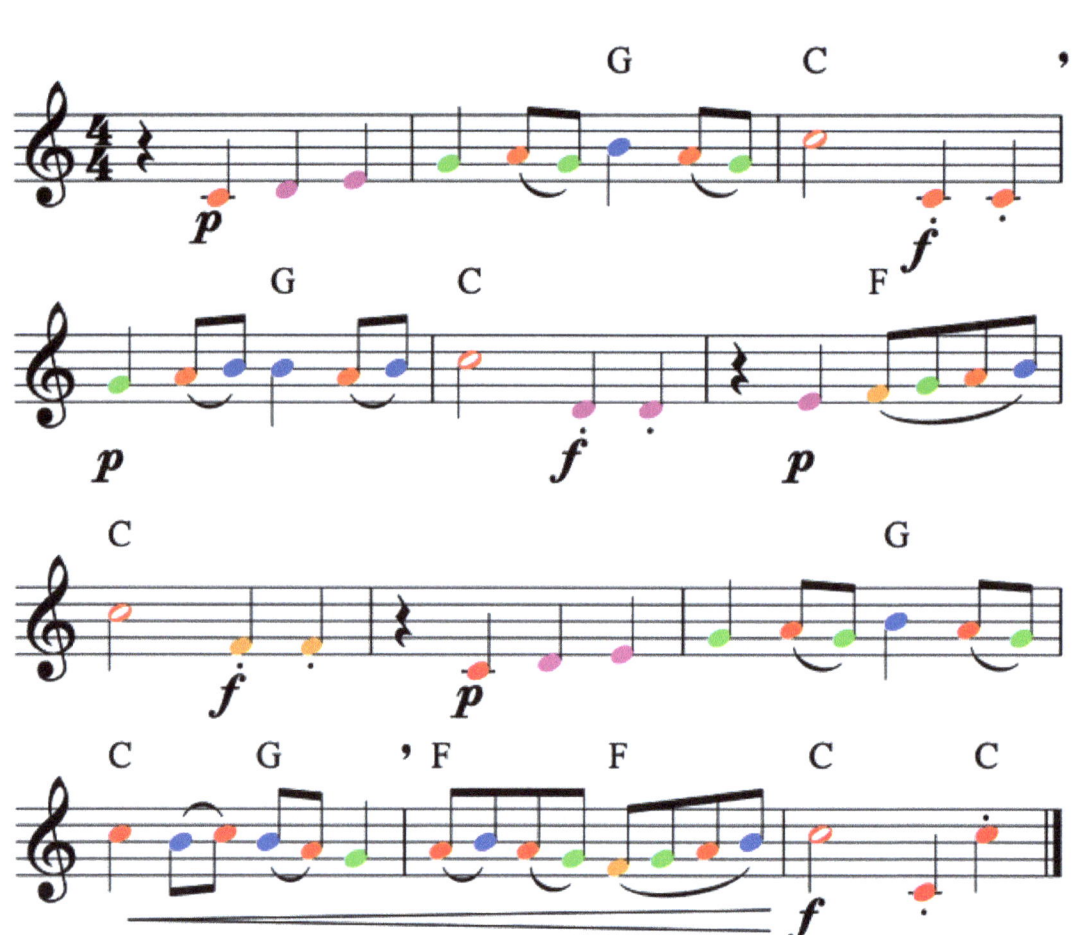

Musical Morning

AS

Let's Celebrate

Congratulations on completing
Toot! Toot! Flute Book 1.

Practice Diary

Name: _____

Date	Homework	Su	Mo	Tu	We	Th	Fr	Sa

www.ingramcontent.com/pod-product-compliance
Lightning Source LLC
Chambersburg PA
CBHW061536010526
44107CB00066B/2886